GROWING UP

# Going to the Hospital

Vic Parker

Heinemann Library
Chicago, Illinois

# H

## www.heinemannraintree.com
Visit our website to find out more information about Heinemann-Raintree books.

## To order:
☎ Phone 888-454-2279
🖥 Visit www.heinemannraintree.com to browse our catalog and order online.

Edited by Dan Nunn, Rebecca Rissman, and Sian Smith
Designed by Joanna Hinton-Malivoire
Picture research by Elizabeth Alexander
Originated by Capstone Global Library Ltd
Printed in the United States of America by
 Worzalla Publishing.

15 14 13 12 11 10
10 9 8 7 6 5 4 3 2 1

**Library of Congress Cataloging-in-Publication Data**
Parker, Victoria.
  Going to the hospital / Vic Parker.
    p. cm.—(Growing up)
  What is a hospital?—Why might I go to a hospital?—What is it like being a patient?—Who will I meet in hospital?—What might happen to me in hospital? —Will anything hurt me at hospital?—Will I have to stay in hospital?—What will happen if I need an operation?—What happens when I leave hospital?—Tips on how to behave in a hospital.
  Includes bibliographical references and index.
  ISBN 978-1-4329-4797-2 (hc)—ISBN 978-1-4329-4807-8 (pb) 1. Children—Preparation for medical care—Juvenile literature. 2. Hospital care—Juvenile literature. 3. Hospitals—Juvenile literature. I. Title.
  R130.5.P374 2011
  362.11—dc22                    2010024191

**Acknowledgments**
We would like to thank the following for permission to reproduce photographs: Alamy pp. 4 (© Jeff Greenberg), 5 (© Photofusion Picture Library), 14, 23 glossary patient (© Blend Images); Corbis pp. 17 (© William Taufic), 18, 23 glossary operation (© Tim Pannell), 19 (© Rubberball), 21, 23 glossary receptionist (© Deborah Jaffe); Getty Images pp. 11 (Christopher Furlong), 13, 23 glossary X-ray (Jonatan Fernstrom/Cultura), 16 (Sean Justice/The Image Bank); iStockphoto p. 8 (© Carmen Martínez Banús); Photolibrary pp. 7 (SW Productions/White), 9, 23 glossary ambulance (Image Source), 10 (ERproductions Ltd/Blend Images), 15 (Image100), 20, 23 glossary ward (Jose Luis Pelaez Inc/Blend Images); Shutterstock pp. 6 (© Monkey Business Images), 12 (© Andresr), 23 glossary stethoscope (© Adrian Grosu).

Front cover photograph of a boy, a doctor, and a toy monkey reproduced with permission of Photolibrary (Laurence Mouton/Photoalto). Back cover photographs of a stethoscope reproduced with permission of Shutterstock (© Andresr), and a patient reproduced with permission of Photolibrary (ERproductions Ltd/Blend Images).

We would like to thank Matthew Siegel for his invaluable help in the preparation of this book.

Every effort has been made to contact copyright holders of material reproduced in this book. Any omissions will be rectified in subsequent printings if notice is given to the publisher.

**Disclaimer**
All the Internet addresses (URLs) given in this book were valid at the time of going to press. However, due to the dynamic nature of the Internet, some addresses may have changed or ceased to exist since publication. While the author and publisher regret any inconvenience this may cause readers, no responsibility for any such changes can be accepted by either the author or the publisher.

# Contents

Some words are shown in bold, **like this**.
You can find them in the glossary on page 23.

# What Is a Hospital?

A hospital is a building where people go to see a special doctor.

Hospitals are very busy places.

A person who goes to a hospital is called a **patient**.

Some patients go in and out of the hospital the same day, but others stay for longer.

# Why Might I Go to a Hospital?

You might go to a hospital to visit a relative or friend who is staying there for a while.

They may have their own room, or be in a room with several other **patients**.

Some patients feel and look much more sick than others.

You can cheer up patients by visiting them.

# What Is It Like Being a Patient?

Sometimes your doctor might ask you to go to the hospital as a **patient**.

You can have special tests there to find out if something is wrong with your body.

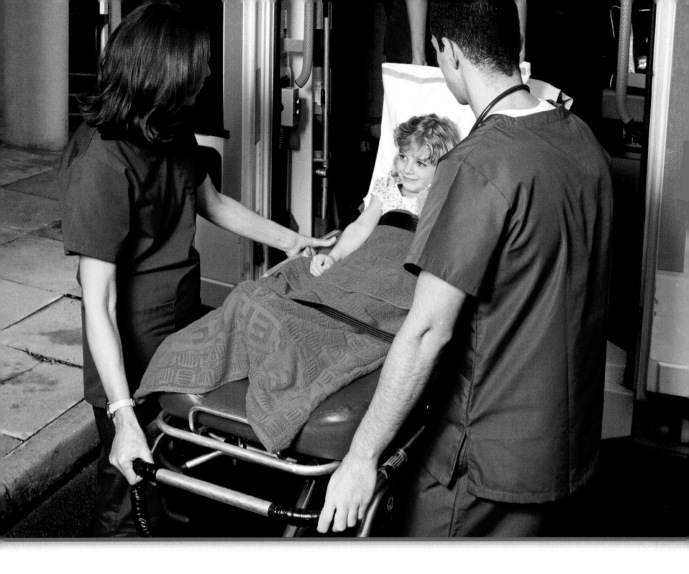

You might also need to go to the
hospital if you have an accident or
become very sick.

You might go there in an **ambulance**.

# Who Will I Meet in the Hospital?

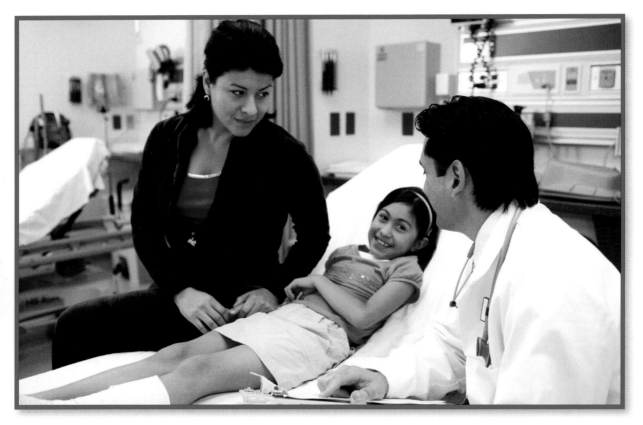

There are lots of people who work in a hospital.

If you are a **patient**, you will see a doctor or a nurse.

There are lots of other people who work in hospitals, too.

There are **receptionists**, cleaners, and more.

# What Might Happen to Me in the Hospital?

stethoscope

The doctors and nurses will sometimes ask lots of questions.

They may want to listen to your chest with a **stethoscope**, or to take your temperature.

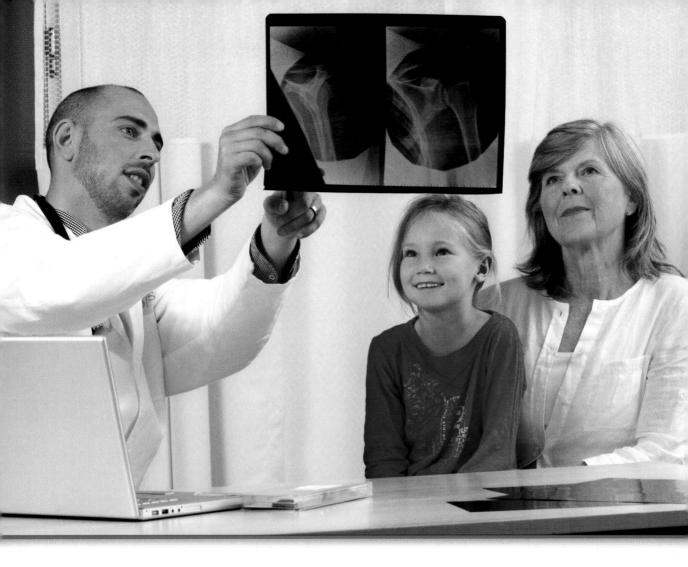

You might go to have special tests done, such as **X-rays**.

An X-ray is a photograph of your bones, so a doctor can see if any are broken.

# How Will I Feel in the Hospital?

Some medical care might be a little unpleasant or uncomfortable.

It is natural to be worried sometimes.

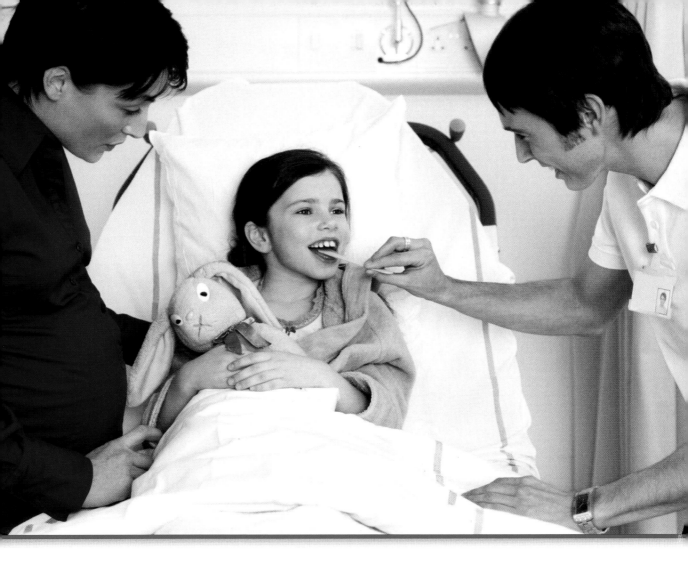

But doctors and nurses are there to take care of you.

They do everything because they are trying to help you and make you better.

# Will I Have to Stay in the Hospital?

Sometimes you have to stay in the hospital for a while.

Your mom, dad, or guardian can stay with you.

In the hospital's children's **unit**, there will be toys you can play with in bed.

If you do not have to stay in bed, you can go to the unit's playroom to play.

# What Will Happen If I Need an Operation?

An **operation** is when doctors try to fix problems inside your body.

Before the operation, they will give you medicine to make you fall asleep.

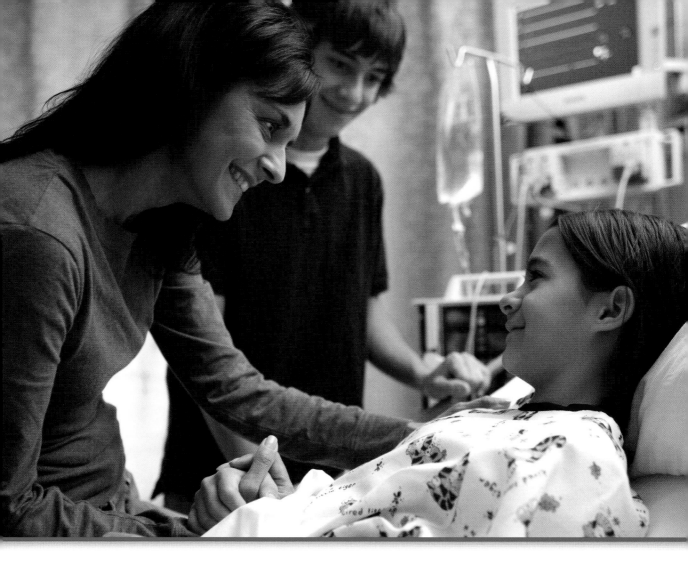

The medicine means you will not feel anything during the operation.

When you wake up, your mom, dad, or guardian will be there with you.

# What Happens When I Leave the Hospital?

When it is time to leave the hospital, you may be given medicine to take with you.

You can take this medicine at home.

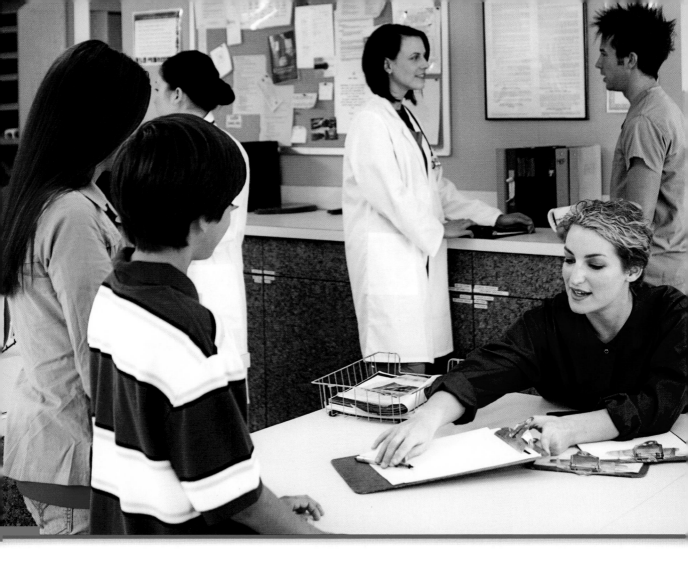

If you need to go back to the hospital
later, you may be given an appointment.

Then you can come and see a doctor
again another day.

# How to Behave in the Hospital

## Dos:

✓ Do wash your hands or use hand-cleaning gel to kill any germs.

✓ Do take a **patient** a get-well card or a small present such as a magazine.

## Don'ts:

✗ Don't visit a patient if you are sick. The patient may catch your illness and become more sick.

✗ Don't use a cell phone. It may disturb people.

# Picture Glossary

 **ambulance** vehicle that is used to take someone who is very sick to the hospital. It has special equipment inside.

 **operation** when a doctor fixes problems inside your body. For most operations, the patient takes medicine that makes them sleep

 **patient** person who goes into the hospital to be made better

 **receptionist** person sitting at a desk near the entrance of a building, who meets people and tells them where to go

 **stethoscope** piece of equipment that a doctor uses to listen to a person's breathing and heartbeat

 **unit** special area in a hospital where certain kinds of patients—for example, children—stay until they get better

 **X-ray** photograph of inside the body

# Find Out More

## Books

Amos, Janine, and Howard Davies. *Going to the Hospital* (Changes). New York: Alphabet Soup, 2010.

Aylmore, Angela. *We Work at the Hospital* (Where We Work). Chicago: Heinemann Library, 2006.

Thomas, Pat. *Do I Have to Go to the Hospital?: A First Look at Going to the Hospital*. Hauppauge, N.Y.: Barrons, 2006.

## Websites

Learn more about being in the hospital at:
**http://kidshealth.org/kid/feel_better/places/hospital.html**

Find out what nurses can do to help patients at:
**http://kidshealth.org/kid/feel_better/people/nurses.html**

# Index